PRIMARY SOURCES
OF
IMMIGRATION AND MIGRATION
IN AMERICA

IMMIGRATION, MIGRATION,

AND THE

GROWTH OF THE AMERICAN CITY

Tracee Sioux

The Rosen Publishing Group's

PowerKids Press
PRIMARY SOURCE

New York

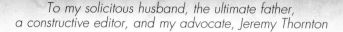

*To my solicitous husband, the ultimate father,
a constructive editor, and my advocate, Jeremy Thornton*

Published in 2004 by The Rosen Publishing Group, Inc.
29 East 21st Street, New York, NY 10010

First Edition

Editor: Rachel O'Connor
Book Design: Emily Muschinske

Photo Credits: Cover, title page, p.4, Picture Collection, The Branch Libraries, New York Public Library, Astor, Lenox and Tilden Foundations; cover and title page (left) © Hulton/Archive/Getty Images; pp. 7 (top), 8 (top), 11 (top), 12 (top), 15 (top), p. 20 (right) © Culver Pictures; pp. 7 (bottom), 8 (bottom), 15 (center), 16 (top), 20 (left), Library of Congress Prints and Photographs Division; pp. 8 (top right), 15 (bottom), 16 (bottom) © Bettmann/Corbis; p. 11 (bottom) © Corbis; p 12 (bottom), Library of Congress Prints and Photographs Division, HAER,RI,4-PAWT,3-8; p. 19 (top) © North Wind Picture Archives; p. 19 (bottom), California State Railroad Museum; p. 20 (top) courtesy U.S. Department of the Interior, National Park Service, Edison National Historic Site.

Sioux, Tracee.
Immigration, migration, and the growth of the American city / Tracee Sioux.
    v. cm. — (Primary sources of immigration and migration in America)
Includes bibliographical references (p.) and index.
Contents: The Industrial Revolution changes America — Factory cities and towns — Life in the cities — Early working conditions — Child labor — Labor unions — The Molly Maguires — Immigrant workers and the railroad — The growth of the American city — City life improves.
ISBN 0-8239-6828-6 (lib. bdg.) — ISBN 0-8239-8954-2 (pbk.)
1. Urbanization—United States—History—Juvenile literature. 2. United States—Emigration and immigration—History—Juvenile literature. 3. Migration, Internal—United States—History—Juvenile literature. [1. Urbanization. 2. United States—Emigration and immigration—History. 3. Migration, Internal.] I. Title. II. Series.
HT123 .S56 2004
307.76'0973—dc21

                                        2003002330

Manufactured in the United States of America

Contents

The Industrial Revolution Changes America

Life in America changed a lot after the Industrial Revolution began in the late 1700s. One of the first signs of industrialization was the building of Samuel Slater's first water-powered textile mill in Rhode Island. America changed from an economy that was based on farming and agriculture to one based on manufacturing. People started to migrate to cities from rural parts of America. Factories were being built in the cities, and there was a huge need for factory workers. In 1790, the five most populated cities in America were Boston, New York, Philadelphia, Charleston, and Baltimore. New York was the largest with about 33,000 people.

This is a busy street along the docks of New York City during the 1800s. By 1890, about 35 percent of Americans were living in cities.

Factory Cities and Towns

Industrialization really began to take hold in the late 1800s. By 1900, three American cities had a population of more than 1 million. They were New York with 3.5 million people, Chicago with 1.7 million, and Philadelphia with 1.3 million. Such growth happened because people already living in America started to move close to the factories in the cities. Also, immigrants arriving in America went to cities to find work. At first, people moved so quickly and in such large numbers that the cities and towns were not ready to house them. Shantytowns, where homes were wooden shacks, sprang up overnight.

The invention of the steamship helped Immigration. Steamships reduced the amount of time the journey across the Atlantic took from three months to less than two weeks. Pictured here are immigrants arriving at Ellis Island in 1906.

Left: *This is an example of a shantytown in New York's Upper West Side in 1894.*

Right: *Immigrant families, such as this Italian family shown here, had to endure poor living conditions.*

Above: *A very busy street in Chicago in 1905 shows just how crowded the cities became.*

Life in the Cities

Industrialization brought more jobs and helped the building of cities, but it also created poor living conditions. In many places, sewer systems had not been developed, so garbage and human waste ran in the streets' gutters. Immigrants from the same country usually lived together in neighborhoods, practicing their customs and religions. Many of the immigrants who arrived in America lived in tenement housing in the poor areas of the cities. From about 1865 to 1885, immigrants came mainly from England, Ireland, and Germany to find work and to escape poverty. They did not realize that life in America could be so hard.

This is a photograph of San Francisco in the 1850s. The population at this time was about 30,000.

Early Working Conditions

When immigrants entered America, they usually did not have much money. Most worked in the factories and the coal mines. Wages were usually low and the working hours were long. The air in the factories was often poisonous from various chemicals. It was not uncommon for workers to pass out from exhaustion. Some workers' toes froze off because factories were rarely heated in the winter. During the 1830s and 1840s, factory workers worked 16 to 18 hours each day, 6 days per week. Safety standards were unheard of, and fires sometimes occurred. Coal mining was also a hard, unsafe, and sometimes deadly occupation.

Above: This is what a busy factory during the Industrial Revolution might have looked like. Rows of women worked 10- to 12-hour days in textile factories such as this one.

Right: Here workers are shown in the coal mines of Pennsylvania.

Above: Many young children worked in factories in the late 1800s.

Left: Samuel Slater built the first water-powered textile mill in Rhode Island, pictured here. Slater hired mostly children to work for him. In 1830, 55 percent of the mill workers in Rhode Island were children.

Child Labor

The use of child labor was common in industrial America. Children usually worked 16-hour days for $1 per week. Factory owners liked to hire children. Children were paid less than adults, and their hands were small enough to work the machines in the factories. During this time, children often helped to support the family. Before industrialization, immigrant and migrant children had worked hard to help their parents on farms. It therefore seemed natural for children to work when families moved from farms to cities. However, the children were treated badly in the factories. They were often beaten and were always overworked. In 1938, the Fair Labor Standards Act ended child labor.

Labor Unions

Many factory owners and industrialists profited from overworking and underpaying immigrant workers in their factories and mines. These workers began to rebel against the terrible conditions. During the 1800s, workers started labor unions to fight for their rights. The main issues were safety, working conditions, wages, and the length of the workday. One of the first unions was the Knights of Labor, started in 1869 by nine tailors in Philadelphia. In 1886, Samuel Gompers organized the American Federation of Labor (AFL). It was a national organization of trade unions. The Industrial Workers of the World, also known as the Wobblies, was formed in 1905.

This photograph from 1914 shows a rally run by the Wobblies in support of strikers in Colorado.

Left: *The founders of the Knights of Labor kept their union a secret so that they would not be fired from their jobs.*

Right: *Samuel Gompers founded the AFL. The AFL used strikes to get better contracts and conditions for workers.*

Attention Workingmen!

GREAT

MASS-MEETING

TO-NIGHT, at 7.30 o'clock,

AT THE

HAYMARKET, Randolph St, Bet. Desplaines and Halsted.

Good Speakers will be present to denounce the latest atrocious act of the police, the shooting of our fellow-workmen yesterday afternoon.

Workingmen Arm Yourselves and Appear in Full Force!

THE EXECUTIVE

Above: *This poster advertises a mass meeting for May 4, 1868, to protest the shooting of strikers. Thousands of people gathered at the meeting. When police tried to break up the crowd, someone threw a bomb, killing several police officers. Right: Mary Harris Jones, known as Mother Jones, was a well-known labor leader.*

Unpopular Unions

During the early 1900s, laws were passed that improved conditions for workers. For example, the average working day was reduced to eight hours. However, most unions that formed during this period either failed or did not become strong until later in the twentieth century. Unions were unpopular because union strikes and occasional conflict unsettled city life.

The Molly Maguires were a group of Irish immigrant coal miners who walked out of the coal mines in 1875. The mine owners brought in forces to break through the strike, and things turned fierce. The Molly Maguires were arrested and 10 were hanged. This event led to anti-union feelings throughout the country.

Immigrant Workers and the Railroad

Industrial America and its cities were able to grow quickly because of the huge amount of immigrants who came to be part of the workforce. The movement of immigrants to cities, and of people migrating from the country, was aided by the development of the railroad. One immigrant group in particular, the Chinese, was very important in the building of the Central Pacific Railroad. The building of railroads was necessary for industry in America to grow. It allowed the goods manufactured by the factories to be brought in and out of cities and towns. Railroads grew from 35,000 miles (56,327 km) of track in 1865 to about 242,000 miles (389,461 km) in 1900.

Above: In 1897, there were five railroads that crossed America. Cities such as Chicago, Illinois, and Dallas, Texas, became important transportation centers. Los Angeles, California, grew quickly after railroads connected it to the East Coast.

Right: Immigrant laborers work on the Southern Pacific Railroad.

Left: *Sources of light in cities went from candles to gas lamps to electric lightbulbs.*

The Woolworth Building (sketch, above) was the world's tallest building until the Chrysler Building was completed in 1930.

Growth of the American City

As industry grew, cities became known for what they produced. Houston, Texas, made railroad cars. Birmingham, Alabama, manufactured steel, and Toledo, Ohio, made glass. New technologies helped to change the look of the industrialized city. Buildings could be built taller because of the use of iron, and later steel, supports in construction. The invention of passenger elevators in 1853 also allowed for taller buildings. In 1885, the first steel-frame skyscraper was erected in Chicago. In 1913, the 60-story Woolworth Building was built in New York. Transportation within cities developed from walking or traveling by horse to riding in electric streetcars.

The Chicago Opera House, pictured here in the 1890s, is an example of the architecture that was taking hold in America's cities.

City Life Improves

Despite the hardships caused by the rapid growth of American cities, improvements came quickly. The lives of immigrant and migrant workers began to improve as work laws changed and advances in technology helped the cities to grow. Roads, railroads, streetcars, sewer systems, and garbage collection became available.

As working and housing conditions improved, an increasing number of people of similar social and economic classes were able to migrate to the same neighborhoods. City life also provided cultural opportunities. The theater, social clubs, movie houses, and stores made cities exciting places to be.

Glossary

cultural (KUL-chuh-rul) Having to do with the beliefs, practices, and arts of a group of people.

customs (KUS-tumz) Practices common to many people in an area or a social class.

developed (dih-VEH-lupt) Worked out in great detail.

gutters (GUH-turz) Sewers along the side of a street.

hardships (HARD-ships) Events or actions that cause suffering.

immigrants (IH-muh-grints) People who move to a new country from another country.

Industrial Revolution (in-DUS-tree-ul reh-vuh-LOO-shun) A time in history beginning in the mid-1700s, when power-driven machines were first used to produce goods in large quantities.

migrate (MY-grayt) To move from one place to another.

occupation (ah-kyoo-PAY-shun) The kind of work a person does.

poverty (PAH-ver-tee) The state of being poor.

rally (RA-lee) A large gathering of people who come together for a common purpose.

rural (RUR-ul) In the country or in a farming area.

rebel (ruh-BEL) To disobey the people or country in charge.

sewer systems (SOO-er SIS-temz) Underground pipes that carry waste.

strikes (STRYKS) Refusals to work until changes are made.

tenement (TEN-uh-ment) A building with many floors and with many families living on each level.

textile (TEK-styl) Woven fabric or cloth.

Index

Primary Sources

Cover. Construction of street railroads. Barclay Street, New York. October 14, 1891. **Inset.** A poster, featuring the Statue of Liberty, telling immigrants they can "earn more" and "learn more" in the United States. **Page 4.** Along the docks of New York City. 1800s. **Page 7. Top.** "Squatters." Shantytown at Amsterdam Avenue and 100th Street in New York City. 1894. **Bottom.** Immigrants arriving at Ellis Island on the ship SS *Patricia*. 1906. **Page 8. Top center.** Italian immigrants, Chicago. Photograph by Lewis Hine (1874–1940). **Top right.** Traffic jam at a street intersection in Chicago. 1905. **Bottom.** View of San Francisco harbor. Daguerreotype, circa 1850s. **Page 15. Top.** Founders of the Knights of Labor. 1886. **Center.** Photograph of Samuel Gompers (1850–1924). Gompers, a cigar maker by trade, was president of the American Federation of Labor. The AFL had a membership of about two million. **Bottom.** Industrial Workers of the World meeting in sympathy with the Laidlaw, Colorado, strikers. Alex Berkman speaking at the rally. May 1, 1914. **Page 16. Top.** Poster for the Haymarket mass meeting. 1886. **Bottom.** Labor leader Mary Harris Jones, known as Mother Jones. Photograph, 1918. **Page 19. Bottom.** Chinese laborers working on the Southern Pacific Railroad, on the line between Bakersfield and Los Angeles. They are posed aboard a hand car. Circa mid-1870s. **Page 20. Top center.** Thomas Edison's electric lamp. Circa 1890–1920. **Left.** Graphite sketch of the Woolworth Building by Cass Gilbert. 1910. **Right.** The Chicago Opera House. Photograph by J. W. Taylor. 1890s.

Web Sites

Due to the changing nature of Internet links, PowerKids Press has developed an online list of Web sites related to the subject of this book. This site is updated regularly. Please use this link to access the list:

www.powerkidslinks.com/psima/amecity/